NOW

Spiritual Discernment for Cultural Encounters

WHAT?

DR. GARY L. GREEN

Carpenter's Son Publish.

Now What? Spiritual Discernment for Cultural Encounters

© 2013 by Gary L. Green

Published by Carpenter's Son Publishing, Franklin, Tennessee

Cover and Interior Design by Suzanne Lawing

Edited by Robert Irvin

Printed in the United States of America

978-0-9885931-8-3

Table of Contents

To my wife Frances – whose love, friendship, and encouragement have blessed me through many moments of discernment.

FOREWORD

Dr. Gary Green's *Now What?: Spiritual Discernment for Cultural Encounters* offers a gentle yet exceptional insight into knowing a call to missions and ministry. If you choose not to engage in "overseas" missions, the penetrating narratives and well-built reflections will nevertheless help create self-awareness and where you should be in the best of self-reflective traditions. The author's credibility and life journey should not be minimized, for his experiences enrich the interpretation. His voyage to missions began with conviction for something compelling, something beyond his lucrative private practice in veterinary medicine. He later earned a graduate degree in religion; this helped him develop his talents to facilitate church leadership and better contribute to the needs of others. Today, his calling persists as missions professor, encourager, personal coach, and developer of short- and long-term missions to hundreds.

Dr. Green galvanizes his decision experience and extends it to help readers visualize how one's calling works—and the things that must be considered alongside that calling. His skillful weaving of narratives, examples, and Scriptures enlarge one's perspective, energize decision-making, and surprisingly awaken a sense of one's future, regardless of final vocation. You may find it hard to put the book down—I wanted to continue the chapters and I felt led through the fascinating reflections and pathways that clarify both feelings and knowledge.

To use Gary's words: this book will help you *connect the dots.* You'll discover spiritual and inner resources that range from the challenge to look backward, for a time, to the call to look forward and await creative gifts for the future. The reading is easy, the thoughts challenging, the feelings moving, and no one will be disappointed.

> **Dr. Carley Dodd**
> *Dean, Graduate School, Abilene Christian University; Author of 12 books; Founder, Go Culture International*

Chapter 1

NOW WHAT?

I was ending my second year of veterinary school when an opportunity came my way to visit Venezuela. I decided to use the trip to investigate ways to serve as a vocational missionary after graduation. However, I was not well prepared for all that would happen.

After the adrenaline rush of flying for the first time and leaving the country for the first time, I settled in for a short stay with the local missionary. I shadowed him in his mentoring time, group studies, and visits. A whole world opened up before me—which was probably not that big of an occurrence since I was a sheltered country boy. I saw and heard how God changed lives, started new communities, and transformed families. I visited with a preacher who had been a gang member, spoke with a missionary who had dropped out of school to follow his calling, and heard high school students speak deeply of faith. When I finally visited two veterinary schools, working in medicine was not nearly as exciting as it once had seemed.

The last night in the missionary's home put me over the edge. Basically, he urged me to return—and ASAP—to be a part of the local work. "Forget school; you already know all you need. I'll help you find the funding. Just come back and help us," he said. When I finally boarded the plane, my head was spinning with all the options. Was God speaking through this man? Should I take this as a sign that God was confirming my vocational missions idea? Maybe God was calling me to drop out of vet school to pursue work in church planting? Was this an open door to missions and a closed door to medicine? Or was this a test? I had pursued medicine for years. Now that I was two years away from this coveted goal, would it be wise—or, his will—to cast aside all that I had accomplished and the efforts put into me by others? My head was swimming with questions about how to process the experience.

In an effort to gain more insight I sought advice from my parents, elders, and peers. The feedback was as broad as the horizon. I spent time in prayer but never felt like I had clear direction. What was I supposed to do?

Maybe you are in a similar phase of life right now. You have experienced a time in which you saw God, others, and yourself in new ways. The question you now face is what to do with these experiences. Is God giving you new direction or reinforcing older ideas? Should you make adjustments in your future plans due to what you have experienced? What do the people closest to you think about what you have gone through?

What is God's will for your life now?

Chapter 2

HIS WILL, MY LIFE

"This, then, is how you should pray: 'Our Father in heaven, hallowed be your name, your kingdom come, your will be done, on earth as it is in heaven.'" MATTHEW 6:9, 10

Going a little farther, he fell with his face to the ground and prayed, "My Father, if it is possible, may this cup be taken from me. Yet not as I will, but as you will." MATTHEW 26:39

Jesus' ministry was framed by a desire to do God's will, and all true followers of Jesus cultivate that same desire. The rub comes in figuring out exactly what his will is. In most cases of decision making, we are not concerned about his sovereign will for the universe or his moral will for humankind, but rather, we desire to find out his *specific will for my life*. Should I assume that his will is planted in my heart and will somehow guide my thoughts so that the plans I make are really his plans? Or should I be watching for intangible signs and waiting for gentle nudges in my heart? Maybe his will only comes through the voices of others in my life? Or maybe his will was written down once and for all, and everything else is simply applying those principles to my situation. The theories are abundant; the questions are confusing.

> Or maybe his will was written down once and for all, and everything else is simply applying those principles to my situation. The theories are abundant; the questions are confusing.

If we survey the literature, there are basically three major schools of thought regarding how to know God's will—the dot theory, the ditch theory, and the dad theory. Not everyone calls them by those names, but using the three Ds makes them a little easier to remember.

The **dot theory**, also often called the bull's-eye principle, is basically the idea that God's will is set for each of us. If I believe that God has a specific plan for my individual life, then I believe the dot theory. The concept is that God knows me personally and has predetermined how I should live. He has an exact person picked out for me to marry, a job lined up that I should take, a place where I am to live, and so on. This way of viewing God's will is comforting in the sense that it makes the transcendent, sovereign God who controls the universe seem more personal and intimate. My role in the relationship is to figure out what he has already predetermined. Since his will is specific to my life, then I must watch for specific signs and guidance. The closer I get to his predetermined will, the more joyful and full my life will be—sort of like the closer I get to the bull's-eye, the more points I get.

This is also where problems pop up.

A major issue with the dot theory is that it produces incredible anxiety. In my desire to get it right and experience all that God has planned, fear takes over. What if I miss the mark? What if I misunderstand? If I marry the wrong person, am I now off track for the rest of my life? If I take the wrong job or move to the wrong town, am I then outside the will of God? Is it possible to ever get back to his plan, or have I now taken a detour that will never be as good as the original plan? This means that the stakes are ridiculously high for each decision.

Most people would rather not risk such an error and, therefore, put off all decision making until something happens to give them absolute certainty. Life, however, rarely gives us certainty, and often opportunities are missed due to hesitancy. Were those opportunities the ones that I should have taken? Anxiety is a natural by-product of the dot theory.

In addition, living by the dot theory requires me to be very astute to interpreting the signs around me. Distinguishing between chance, consequence, and a sign from God can be difficult. Asking for a sign also becomes quite common. This contributes even more anxiety to the decision-making process. In reality, living by signs is perhaps more equivalent to living by sight than living by faith. Though it may feel very spiritual, it may actually work against our faith development.

Some people are not paralyzed by the dot theory but rather live in a more ambivalent manner. Taking the dot theory to its logical conclusion nurtures this attitude. If God does have a plan for every person that he has predetermined, then basically we are saying that the future is set. If the future is set, then I really don't have to make an effort to figure out God's will, since any action I take must have been the action that God predetermined. In essence, I cannot *not* do his will if everything is predetermined. If that is the case, then decision making requires no effort on my part.

Thus two extremes are frequently precipitated by the

dot theory—anxiety over the littlest decision, or ambivalence to all decisions.

If we reject the concept that God has predetermined all of life—if we choose the theology of Jacob Arminius over that of John Calvin—then we must pursue a new viewpoint regarding the understanding of God's will. One option is to see God as unconcerned with the details of our lives and primarily concerned with morality. As long as we avoid moral failures—i.e., sin—we are pretty much free to do as we choose. Thus the idea is that life is like a road of morality with ditches on both sides. My job is to navigate life in such a way that I stay on the road and out of the ditches of sin. As long as I stay out of the ditch, God will be happy with the outcome. Hence, we get the name: the *ditch theory*. In other words, I have total freedom in decision making as long as my decisions do not result in sin for others or myself.

> In other words, I have total freedom in decision making as long as my decisions do not result in sin for others or myself.

As you can imagine, this viewpoint is quite freeing for many people. Rather than seek out the one plan of God for this one moment in my life, suddenly I have options. I can choose from a wide variety of possibilities. The only anxiety that comes into play here is the anxiety of choosing between multiple options of varying value.

Yet, valid objections can be raised regarding the ditch theory. Is God really only a moral referee? Is the role of judge the only role he plays in my life? The Sermon on the Mount calls the followers of Jesus to be proactive, to live in love, and to change the world. Scripture teaches about relationships, family, money, honor, and all aspects of life. To limit God's will to only the margins of life is to ignore the bulk of Scripture and even ignore much of the driving force of the incarnation.

So while it seems that the dot theory overly involves God in each step of life, the ditch theory under-involves God in each step of life.

Personally, I favor a third option—the ***dad theory.***

As the father of four children who are all now in high school or above, I hold great hopes for my children's futures. Yet I refuse to micromanage or be a hovering parent. (In the last decade, they even came up with a popular tag for such moms and dads: *helicopter parents.*) My children must learn to make choices and live with the consequences. However, I refuse to limit my role to only that of a moral referee pointing out bad decisions but doing little more.

As a parent, I often have a broader view of the potential that lies within each child than the child does. From our relationship of many years, I have grown a deep understanding of the latent abilities that lie within each and can see how different situations will be either beneficial or detrimental. Thus, my role now is to guide my children to choose well from a variety of options so that he or she can be fulfilled and mature. As long as the option leads my child to the joy of living well for self and others, I will be proud.

This is very similar to coaching in sports. Like a coach, I give direction or withhold it depending upon what is best in the moment. Like a coach, I know that each player is different and will perform differently. As long as their performance uses their abilities well and they grow toward maturity, I will be content. Likewise, God as a parent offers us counsel, wisdom, and help as we play the game of life. It is rare that he directly intervenes, but that does not mean he is unconcerned. Rather, he allows us to exercise our free will and is pleased with any decision we make that leads us to fulfillment and maturity.

If we take all three viewpoints and walk through a decision-making situation, the importance of recognizing which viewpoint I hold becomes clear. Let's take the example of Sharon.

Sharon is a pre-law major because she wants to advocate social justice in the world. However, she is not convinced that law is the only way to express her deep desires; she is interested in many different ways of serving others. She just had a challenging internship for the summer followed by an unexpected event when she returned home. In the weeks between her internship and returning to school, a friend told her that she should consider opening a business. Sharon is smart and comes from a family that has had great success in business. Her friend contends that not many people will be as successful in business as Sharon would be; thus, she should pursue business so that she can give generously to social work and humanitarian efforts. Sharon is struggling with how to proceed.

Her thought process can be governed by one of the following questions. Did God put this person in her life at this moment with this message? If so, she must obey—this is the dot theory. Does it matter to God what she does as long as she does not sin while pursuing either option? If so, she has total freedom to do whatever she wants (the ditch theory). Will God be happy if she chooses law, business, missions, or something else as long as she chooses a career that will allow her to use the gifts he gave her in great ways? If so, then she has options, but those should be greatly influenced by considering the gifts and desires that God has placed inside of her as a unique individual—this is the dad theory.

Sharon's basic belief regarding understanding the will of God can cause her to immediately obey a suggestion, do what she pleases, or continue seeking guidance. It is critical that Sharon come to grips with her core belief regarding the will of God.

Returning to the example from my own life of deciding between missions and continuing vet school gives us another case to consider. If I had held to the dot theory, then it would have been easy to believe that the invitation from the missionary to join in his work, coupled with my own deep stirrings to serve in missions and my fatigue from vet school, were all part of a direct communication from God. Based on the dot theory, the logical conclusion would have been to have left vet school and moved to the mission field.

If I had held to the ditch theory, then I would have believed that God was not really concerned with my decision. I was free to choose to continue school, move to another country, or just about anything else as long as I did not hurt someone or sin in the process.

If I held to the dad theory, then I would have prayed for more insight into how my desires and gifts connected with this opportunity. Furthermore, I would have sought advice from those who knew me best, and reviewed Scripture for guidance. Only after considering my gifts, advice from others, and Scripture would I have felt good about making a decision since all of those would help me realize how to live in a mature way that produces faith, hope, and love.

Just to set the record straight, I followed the dad theory and was stunned by the advice. I prayed constantly for insight and read Scripture to see how others handled decisions. Multiple people counseled me to stay in school since it would facilitate a better life.

I was told that not many people had the ability I had to be a doctor. Then I consulted with a friend who was in school with me. He bluntly stated that I owed it to all those who had helped me get to this point to finish what I had started. He continued, saying that my presence in vet school meant that someone else who had worked equally as hard was not allowed into the school. Would it be just to disrespect all the money, time, and effort poured into me by family and teachers just to leave a place open that no one would be allowed to fill? Why not achieve the goal that so many had helped me progress toward and then consider what to do? Largely based upon this discussion, I finished school and practiced medicine for two years before moving on to missions. It was a decision that I have never regretted and one I believe honored God, family, and many others while maturing me in significant ways.

So which theory do you live by? Before moving further down this road of decision making, come to grips with this question. Must you read intangible signs properly to recognize what God has predetermined for your specific life? Or is God even concerned with the details of life, and why should you waste time and energy contemplating his will along with your decisions? Or is God taking on the role of a father, in which his desire is for you to mature in faith, hope, and love and use your gifts to the maximum without limiting you to just one option? Which is it for you? Take time and decide before moving on.

REFLECTION

1. Have you found yourself subscribing to *the dot theory*? What decisions have you made in life, to this point, that show you follow this theory? What affect did following the dot theory have on your heart and soul?

2. Have you made decisions following *the ditch theory*? What decisions have you previously made that demonstrate you followed the ditch theory? How did following this theory affect your spiritual life?

3. Do you subscribe to *the dad theory*? What decisions have you made in life, to this point, that show you follow this theory? How did following the dad theory affect your spiritual walk with God?

Chapter 3

EBENEZER

When the Philistines heard that Israel had assembled at Mizpah, the rulers of the Philistines came up to attack them. When the Israelites heard of it, they were afraid because of the Philistines. They said to Samuel, "Do not stop crying out to the Lord our God for us, that he may rescue us from the hand of the Philistines." Then Samuel took a suckling lamb and sacrificed it as a whole burnt offering to the Lord. He cried out to the Lord on Israel's behalf, and the Lord answered him.

While Samuel was sacrificing the burnt offering, the Philistines drew near to engage Israel in battle. But that day the Lord thundered with loud thunder against the Philistines and threw them into such a panic that they were routed before the Israelites. The men of Israel rushed out of Mizpah and pursued the Philistines, slaughtering them along the way to a point below Beth Kar.

Then Samuel took a stone and set it up between Mizpah and Shen. He named it Ebenezer, saying, "Thus far the Lord has helped us." 1 SAMUEL 7:7-12

In this story, Samuel and the nation of Israel experienced a major God-encounter. Following the event, they stopped and raised a monument. This marker served to remind everyone of how God had stepped into his or her life in a significant way. It would be impossible to pass the stone and not reflect on the event and its significance. The stone was named Ebenezer, or "stone of help."

> Yet, life continues and we become busy with other things. Those events can become lost in our memory.

Often in life, we have major experiences that seem transformative and unforgettable in the moment. Yet, life continues and we become busy with other things. Those events can become lost in our memory. Our minds can only process so much information, and research indicates that our minds typically work with only the most recently acquired information. In other words, we are wired so that what is urgent often takes priority over what is important. This means that major events, even God-encounters, frequently have much less effect on our lives than we care to admit.

One way to avoid the loss of the effect of significant events is to name them and reflect on them. By clearly identifying and defining an event, we give it the opportunity to move to a deeper level of consciousness in our hearts and heads.

Clear examples of this can be seen on the mall in Washington D.C. A memorial to our first president, to the president who saved the union, and to the thousands who fell during World War II to preserve our freedom sit at the very heart of our capital. Very appropriately, the Freedom Wall of the WWII memorial has an inscription that reads, "Here We Mark The Price Of Freedom." These memorials mark significant events that we never want to forget. Our nation's leaders saw fit to build these memorials in order to cement into the national memory some of the most important moments and people in our history.

An example in my own life occurred while on the mission field. My wife encouraged me several times to keep a journal. Being much younger and less wise than I am now, I would always reply, "There is no way I will forget this." As is often the case, she was right and I was wrong.

However, after one significantly painful and transformative experience, I took considerable time to process my thoughts and then combined the three lessons I had learned into one image. We then took that image and had it made into a medallion. Most days, I wear the medallion around my neck to remind me of the lessons learned about priorities, balance, and prayer. Whenever I move and it bumps my body or I see the chain in the mirror, I am reminded of the events and their significance.

Some might have been Ebenezer moments where God stepped into your life in amazing ways. Others might have been Ebenezer moments in the life of someone close to you.

Recently, you have experienced life in new ways. Some moments have been encouraging, while others were less so. Some might have been Ebenezer moments where God stepped into your life in amazing ways. Others might have been Ebenezer moments in the life of someone close to you. If your spiritual eyes were open, odds are that God moved in some significant way, or ways, during this time of vulnerability in your life.

Now is the time to raise your own Ebenezer in order

to prevent that moment from being lost to you.

REFLECTION

1. How did you see God during your recent experience? Don't worry about comparing your moments with those of others; this is about you and God. Did you see him in adversity, in victory, in the lives of others, or in your own life? There might be numerous events or there might be only one. Take time now to write about these times.

2. Perhaps there were multiple lesser moments, but one that now overshadows the rest. Your goal is to name that moment. Identify it and write down what happened; simply record the moment for history. If you wrote about it in the first question, then expound upon it here by filling in details such as emotions, the reactions of others, etc. Again, how did you see God during your recent experience?

3. What does this moment mean? What is its significance? How does it affect you or how should it affect you?

4. Write out one short and clear sentence that explains what you have learned.

Chapter 4

THERE WE SAW
THE GIANTS

" . . . all the people that we saw in it are men
of a great stature. And there we saw the giants,
the sons of Anak, which come of the giants . . . "
Numbers 13:32, 33 (KJV)

Historically, there is a lot of guesswork mixed with
scholarship regarding who these people were. At a
minimum, we gather from the report that they made
a significant impression on the spies. The result of the
spies' encounter with these amazing people was such

that they believed the entire nation should ignore the direct promises of God and either retreat to slavery in Egypt or be satisfied with the desert nomad lifestyle. So despite the fact that we cannot all agree on who these giants were, we can all agree that they made a significant impact on the Jewish spies.

> So despite the fact that we cannot all agree on who these giants were, we can all agree that they made a significant impact on the Jewish spies.

During your time in another culture, you came into contact with a wide range of people; some of them seemed like spiritual giants. (OK, for a few of you "height-challenged" people, they might have seemed like giants physically, but let's stay focused on the spiritual side here.) When we come into contact with significant people, we should stop to name or recognize them. If we fail to do so, their significance will weaken over time and the opportunity for growth will be lost. Yet if we stop to recognize what just happened, we can be blessed to embrace the experience as a formative moment.

Often, we know in our heads how we should live, but due to a lack of spiritual giants in our lives, we may never see an example of what mature spirituality looks like. When teaching the Old Testament, I frequently ask students who they know that has faith like the men in the book of Daniel. The overwhelming majority replies "no one." We want to grow and be different, but our lack of walking with people more mature than ourselves thwarts our ability to be transformed.

In Latin America there is an old quote that says, "Tell me with whom you walk and I will tell you who you are." Walking with a spiritual giant can be transformative, but only when we give the experience the right to take root in our hearts. Once we take the time to incorporate the experience into our own spiritual vision, then we can become different people.

In my life I can point to several spiritual giants who have changed me. As a child, I often heard my dad use this phrase: "It ain't bragging if you can do it." Later I found out that Dad was quoting the baseball player Dizzy Dean. However, when you hear it a number of times from the mouth of your dad, it becomes part of who you are. Combine that with my overachieving tendencies, and you end up with a pretty prideful young man. It was then that I met Jimmy.

Jimmy Carter was an elder in our church. At first I was impressed just because he had the same name as our 39th president, but then I got to know the man. What I initially did not understand was why he was an elder in our church. Other elders were much more "apt to teach" and possessed obvious leadership skills as bankers, investors, and professors. Jimmy, on the other hand, was a quiet construction worker. I liked the man personally, but struggled with why he would ever be named an elder.

One day I was helping someone move and we needed to borrow a truck. Jimmy owned a heavy-duty pickup and I was encouraged to ask his permission to borrow it. He graciously agreed and I picked it up at the designated time. While stopped at a traffic light, I noticed a legal pad on the seat next to me. The pad had a hand-drawn weekly calendar on the front. I quickly realized it was Jimmy's personal day planner. My first thought was that this seemed so appropriate for a man given to engineering and construction. No fancy day planner in a leather bound binder, just a hand-drawn chart on a legal pad.

It was also about this time that my conscience began to talk to me. It whispered something about privacy and respect, but I ignored the thought and slid the pad closer.

The next thing that caught my eye was that his days started at 4 AM! This sixty-year-old man had an hour blocked off every morning for time with God prior to arriving at work at 6 AM.

I then noticed that the early schedule allowed him to finish work early as well. Every evening, except for one, was filled with the names of people to visit. The other evening simply said "church" on Wednesday night. There must have been twenty names on that list that Jimmy was to visit after work and on the weekend.

It was then and there that I repented of my prideful judgment of Jimmy as an elder. Who better to lead a flock than someone who spent every evening in the homes of those members? Who would I rather follow: a gifted speaker and business leader or a man who rose early to be with God and came to my house late to be with me? My perspective of Jimmy was forever changed and a new vision of living humbly for God was born.

> Most of all, I will never forget the night that his humility not only stunned me but also prevented a church split.

Years later, I also came to realize that I was walking with a spiritual giant in Venezuela. Wilfredo was almost seventy when he came to our church. I thought I was helping him, but later learned how much he was helping me.

Like Jimmy, Wilfredo rose very early each day to spend time in prayer and the Word. He then worked for eight hours as a carpenter in the hundred-degree heat of our city. It made him amazingly strong physically— our university men all confessed that they wanted to have Wilfredo's physique—but it also made him a spiritual giant. Most of all, I will never forget the night that his humility not only stunned me but also prevented a church split.

Wildredo, Daniel, and I were meeting with a middle-aged leader of our church whose pride had been offended. As the meeting moved along, it became clear that he was not with us in order to repent, but that his real purpose was to threaten us with "taking his followers and moving on." His pride had inflamed his anger and he was talking boldly, rashly, and authoritatively about splitting the church. I was doing all I could to stay calm and not match anger with anger. The room fell silent as I searched for words and the right tone for a response. Should I call him out on his pride? Should I confront him bluntly with Scripture? Could I do it without being as angry as he was? Then I saw Wilfredo begin to move.

From his metal folding chair in the circle, Wilfredo leaned to his left with his head slightly bowed until he was within a couple of feet of the other man's face. He looked up at the brother from a submissive position and then said in the most genuine and gentle voice, "Brother, I don't think I'd be threatening to take people to hell with you, if I were you." Slowly, he resumed his normal sitting position and simply looked straight ahead. After a brief moment of silence, the man broke down in tears and repented. Wilfredo put his arm around the man and gently said, "It's alright. It happens to us all from time to time."

In that moment, I wanted to be Wilfredo. I wanted to be that genuine and gentle. I wanted to be able to turn anger into repentance, hate into love. I was and still am inspired by my friend, the spiritual giant Wilfredo.

So what is your story? Who are the giants you have seen?

REFLECTION

1. Write down the story of your encounter with a spiritual giant or giants. Include the details of time, place, and feelings. What did that person do that inspired you?

2. What characteristics of this spiritual giant(s) do you want to imitate in your life? How could you pursue them?

3. Again, try to put into one sentence what you have learned from this experience.

Chapter 5

GRASSHOPPERS

The rest of Numbers 13:32 reads:

*"We seemed like grasshoppers in our own eyes,
and we looked the same to them."*

After seeing the giants, the Israelites' view of themselves was significantly changed.

When we have major God-encounters or walk with giants, we suddenly see ourselves differently. It is not that we are different, but our perspective of ourselves is changed. Only by placing self in the shoes of others do we get to see self in a new way. We suddenly see what some others have been seeing all along. This is one of the greatest blessings of cross-cultural ministry—our souls are more vulnerable and the perspectives of others are more available. When we live only within our familiar environment, we might go for years without any new insights about ourselves. Yet when we make ourselves vulnerable, we increase the probability for new insights.

> Over time, in familiar environments, we learn how to cover our faults.

Over time, in familiar environments, we learn how to cover our faults. We might develop other strengths to offset a weakness, avoid situations where our faults are exposed, or limit contact with people that make us face our frailties. When we are in control of our environment, we can successfully dodge the pain of honest introspection. But cross-cultural ministry tends to keep us just a little "out of control." The result is often the painful reality of seeing ourselves as grasshoppers.

Following a particularly painful year of ministry that had left me dry spiritually, I was called "ungrateful" by one of my overseeing deacons. My first reaction was to reject the notion and, honestly, I might have done so outwardly if I only had enough energy. Yet with my emotional and spiritual energy drained, I just let the idea simmer in my heart rather than fight back. Over the next few weeks, I spent time reflecting on how he might have come by his perspective. Later I found myself coming to the conclusion that he was right. I had failed to express my gratitude for the efforts of others. Much behind-the-scenes work had gone unrecognized by me as I barreled along at full speed in my own ministry. Without being in a vulnerable place and receiving the insight of another, I would probably still be offending people today with my lack of gratitude. Rather than continue in my ways, I wrote this deacon a letter expressing gratitude for his insight, and I have since tried to specifically thank people for what they do.

Not all new insights about self have to be painful, though. There is a different way—cross-cultural ministry brings new self-awareness. Often, new settings will require us to experience a new type of ministry or rely on a different gift mix than we are comfortable with. When this happens, we should take the time to recognize it.

It is possible that this new experience will open up a new realm of possibilities for our giftedness. For example, my brother-in-law recently took an administrative position with an international school in Thailand. The position puts him in touch with a large number of missionary families whose children attend the school. As we talked at the end of his first year, he expressed his amazement at the breadth of opportunities and types of mission efforts represented by the families at his school. Due to his new job, an entire new world of opportunities lies before him regarding potential future ministry.

Similarly, years ago when I was in vet school, I let a friend talk me into teaching a high school class and working with the same youth at summer camp. On paper, this looked like a great idea. In fact it was—but not in the way I thought. After spending a semester trying to teach a group of high school students whose interest level was not exactly stellar, and then working at a summer camp, where having fun seemed to be the first five priorities of the day, my tranquility had been replaced with irritability. I was struggling with loving the youth and felt more at ease daydreaming about how I might accidentally lose a few of them on a nature walk!

It was a great experience—not the daydreams, but the youth work in general. The experience helped me realize that despite the opinions of some of my friends, I was not cut out for youth ministry. Rather than invest years of time and effort in trying to serve in a ministry for which I was not gifted, I

So what have you learned about yourself through your experiences? Are there personal characteristics that you now see for the first time? Is there a set of gifts that you did not know you had or perhaps thought you had but do not?

spent six months utilizing a gift set that was deficient for the task at hand. It was a six-month investment that taught me a great deal about my giftedness; this was a small price to pay for a valuable insight.

So what have you learned about yourself through your experiences? Are there personal characteristics that you now see for the first time? Is there a set of gifts that you did not know you had or perhaps thought you had but do not? Seeing ourselves in new ways is extremely valuable regardless of whether we see old deficiencies or new strengths.

REFLECTION

1. What experience(s) have you had that revealed new aspects of yourself? Describe the experience or experiences.

2. What was it that you learned? Why had you not seen this before?

3. What should you do with this new insight? What actions should you take to develop yourself in light of what you have learned?

4. Write one succinct sentence that describes what you have learned—and how it will change you.

Chapter 6

JANUS AND IGNATIUS

In Roman mythology, Janus was the god of beginnings and transitions; thus, he was associated with gates, doorways, calendars, and such. The word January—the month for annual transition—derives its name from him. Usually, Janus is depicted as a god with two faces, one looking backward and one facing forward.

Up to this point, we have been facing backward; we have been reflecting on the past. Now it is time to transition and face forward. It is time to raise questions regarding the significance of the past and how it will help you live in the future. What do all these experiences mean for you? How do you put it together and proceed from here?

As we continue, keep this in mind: spiritual formation always takes priority over spiritual divination. In other words, becoming more like Jesus is always more important than figuring out what to do with my life. Rather than focus on what is God's will for me, I should focus on how these experiences can make me more spiritually mature. Once we are spiritually mature, there is no limit to how or where God can use us.

> Understand this: one joyous experience in another country does not necessarily mean that God is calling you to abandon your choice of major, drop out of school, sell what you have, and move there now.

So understand this: one joyous experience in another country does not necessarily mean that God is calling you to abandon your choice of major, drop out of school, sell what you have, and move there now. It might have implications toward that end, but it might be that he is primarily trying to show you areas in your life that need to change in order to be more like his Son. It might be that you are stirred to consider long-term missions or it might be that you are stirred to be a more grace-filled entrepreneur. If the end result is that you become a missionary, then praise God. If the end result is that you become a more Christlike spouse, parent, and/or businessperson, then equally praise God.

Ignatius of Loyola was a sixteenth-century soldier turned priest. His reflections not only resulted in the founding of the Jesuit order but also have blessed millions who seek to discern how to follow God in their personal lives. The following series of steps from Ignatius's work are designed to help you take what you have learned from your reflections and discern how to move forward in God's will.

A. Deep Desires

One of Ignatius's key concepts was that God speaks to us from within via our deepest desires. These are not the desires for quick pleasures and entertainment but rather those deep desires that give purpose to life. Nurturing these desires leads to growth in faith, hope, and love. When we grow in faith, hope, and love, we become more conformed to the image of Christ.

As followers of Jesus, we believe that God actively communicates with his people. Throughout history he has shown that he is not limited in how he can do this. He has communicated through the written word, other people, writing on a wall, a burning bush, dreams, talking donkeys, and much, much more. Perhaps he has been using the experiences you described at the end of the last chapter to communicate with you. If those experiences have produced faith, hope, and love, then chances are that God was working to speak to your heart and transform your soul.

Thus far you have contemplated how you saw God, others, and yourself in new ways. Does there seem to be a deep desire that is being stirred by these experiences? Does the sum of them move you in a way that causes faith, hope, and love to come alive? For example, if you found that you were inspired to see God care for marginal people, you discovered in yourself a gift mix that was very beneficial to those people, and whenever you reflected on those moments you felt deep joy and hope, then perhaps God is communicating to you that a mature way to use your life would be in the service of the marginal. Or perhaps your experiences have caused you to appreciate spiritually deep communities in ways that you never realized before. Perhaps you experienced deep joy when you served as part of a spiritual family that loved and served each other in an area of the world where life is often not joyful. If so, then perhaps God is stirring your deep desire to work in a similar community or grow in appreciation for the community you are already in.

A word of caution here: let's not jump too quickly from recognizing God at work to setting out on a new course for your entire life. The implications from God's communication deserve careful contemplation. What his message means to one person might be significantly different than what it means to another—and time is required to discern this.

For example, three students might experience the exact same internship, but due to their gift mix and situations in life, the implications of the internship are radically different. Perhaps all served among the same marginal people and were deeply touched by doing so. All feel that God is stirring a desire to use their lives to show compassion for the marginal and to help ease their suffering. For one person this might mean working for a major US corporation and using her business skills and/or personal income to set up a microloan system among the poor. For the second student with a gift mix in exercise science, it could mean serving as a coach to inner-city children. For the last person it might mean returning to the site of the internship in order to live among the poor as a teacher and servant. All experienced the same communication from God that stirred similar desires; the implications, however, are different for each due to their gift mix and background.

For example, three students might experience the exact same internship, but due to their gift mix and situations in life, the implications of the internship are radically different.

How you should nurture the desire that has been stirred in you is the great question you now face and the one we will continue to address. For the moment, your goal is to identify which desire is being stirred. To which area deep within you has God been speaking? Was it related to growth in your character, vocational choice, relationships, missions, or something else?

Goal 1: Deepest Desire(s)

What is the deepest desire(s) that God is inspiring within you, based on your past experiences? The important thing, for now, is to identify that desire, or desires.

Once you have identified the area in your life where God is at work, then you can begin to play loosely with the possible options of how to nurture these desires. As you think creatively about multiple options—and it is important to keep multiple options in your mind at this point—then proceed with these other steps of Ignatian discernment.

REFLECTION

1. What deep desire or desires within you is God stirring? What area of your life has been moved by this experience?

2. What are different ways that you can nurture and develop this desire, or these desires, now that you have completed the experience?

3. Make sure to journal both of these answers (whether using this space or your own journal). It's important to put your thoughts on paper.

B. Prayer

One of the most frustrating things about God is that he doesn't seem to be too preoccupied with conforming to my specific expectations. As a child, Dad told me that we were about to get an NFL franchise in our state. Thus I became a major fan before the New Orleans Saints ever chose their first player. Unfortunately, the franchise did not meet with great success until forty years later. I cannot tell you the number of games I spent praying for a miracle during the '60s, '70s, '80s, and '90s. God just did not seem overly concerned about my team or my emotional state.

Often we feel the same when we face major decisions or try to discern God's will in more important matters. It seems like a big deal to us; so why is he not responding more clearly and urgently? Yet if truth be told, what most of us really want in response to prayer is not what God usually gives.

Jesus' ministry was bookended by two prayers with the same content. In the Sermon on the Mount, he taught us to pray for submission to God's will. In the Garden of Gethsemane, he prayed for his own submission to God's will. So what Jesus focused on was not "what is the next step in my life?" but rather "help me to be submissive to your will." We, on the other hand, often pray for revelation. We really are not as concerned about submitting to the overall plan of God for his kingdom as we are concerned about having direct revelation about what to do next.

> We really are not as concerned about submitting to the overall plan of God for his kingdom as we are concerned about having direct revelation about what to do next.

Solomon prayed at the beginning of his reign that God would give him wisdom. Very rarely do we pray the same. Wisdom implies responsibility and work on our part. What many of us prefer is for God to do all the hard work and just zap us with the "right answer." We prefer to relinquish rather than exercise responsibility.

If we follow the prayer patterns of Jesus and Solomon, then we will be praying for submission to what is best for the kingdom of God and for wisdom to figure it out. With that in mind, it is essential that you take time to talk with God.

Goal 2: Prayer

Make it your goal to pray for submission to God's will—after discerning it as best you can. Remember, the goal is submission, not self-will.

Let this time, and many moments like it over the next few days, be a time to ask for the wisdom to look spiritually, and critically, at the experiences of the past as well as the options for the future.

REFLECTION

1. Does the content of your prayers look like the content of Jesus' prayer in the Sermon on the Mount and in the garden? If not, what attitude and/or petition do you need to change? Be sure to journal that needed change.

2. Spend time now praying for wisdom for future decisions. Ask for success in planning steps that glorify God and produce faith, hope, and love.

C. Scripture

God spoke to Jeremiah about an approaching disaster for Israel. Transition and even chaos loomed on the horizon. When God spoke, he zeroed in on what should be the focus of his people during crisis.

> *This is what the Lord says: "Let not the wise boast of their wisdom or the strong boast of their strength or the rich boast of their riches, but let the one who boasts boast about this: that they have the understanding to know me, that I am the Lord, who exercises kindness, justice and righteousness on earth, for in these I delight," declares the Lord* (JEREMIAH 9:23, 24).

In the case of Jeremiah and pending transition, God said that the focus we should have during transition is not so much clarity for the next step but rather increased depth of spiritual understanding.

Likewise, Jesus rebuked the Pharisees for missing the point when he said in John 5:39, 40, *"You study the Scriptures diligently because you think that in them you have eternal life. These are the very Scriptures that testify about me, yet you refuse to come to me to have life."*

Jesus did not scold the Pharisees for studying Scripture but rather for missing the point when they did study. The goal of Scripture is to lead us to Jesus; it is to bring us back into that relationship with God that Adam and Eve had when they walked with God in the garden in the cool of the day.

Scripture is given to reveal to us the nature of God and lead us into a relationship with him. It teaches me about what pleases or displeases him. It is a record of thousands of relationships with our Creator that should inform me of how to live in relationship with him.

So during days of discernment it would be ridiculous to ignore Scripture, for it is in Scripture that we learn how he responds to integrity or the lack of it. We see how he reacts to fidelity and to broken promises. We learn whom he blesses and why.

As you reflect on the scriptural portrayal of God, turn again to contemplate your future. By now, surely you have some thoughts about how to respond to what you have experienced. This is the time to consider how the God of Scripture might view your potential options.

Goal 3: Scripture

Seek the God of the universe through his Scriptures. Here, you'll hear his heart as well as his voice.

REFLECTION

1. What would be the implications of pursuing the top three options that you have considered for responding to what God has stirred within you? Would they be consistent with his nature? Would they cause you and others to grow in faith, hope, and love? Would the results reflect the nature of God?

2. Can you find examples in Scripture of others who have faced similar decisions? How did God view their plans? Write about one or two.

D. Community

When God created Eve, he also created community. It reflects his nature as the Triune God. If we are to reflect his nature, we need community. None of us individually possesses all the wisdom, gifts, and abilities to reflect Divinity accurately. By living in a spiritual community we come closer to looking like God.

When Jesus faced significant moments of his ministry, he did so in community. He took Peter, James, and John with him

> Who are your garden friends? Who do you want with you in critical moments?

up the Mount of Transfiguration, into the home of the synagogue leader, and deep into the Garden of Gethsemane. These three were closer to him than the other disciples and shared in his most significant moments.

Who are your garden friends? Who do you want with you in critical moments? As you discern the implications of your experiences, let them know your thoughts so that they can walk with you.

One note of wisdom is in order here. At the death of Solomon, his son Rehoboam was faced with a major decision. He consulted the counselors of his father and then consulted his friends. The decision he made was based upon the feedback of his peers, who lacked the insights of the older generation. The result would permanently split the country into two kingdoms.

Goal 4: Community

We all need garden friends; we all need community. Who in your life can help you discern these important questions and guide you through your decisions?

As you consult the community around you, do not make the same mistake that Rehoboam made. Talk with older mentors who have walked this road before. Consider family members and leaders who know you and who you respect. They will have your best interest at heart and will be able to draw upon wisdom from experiences that you have not had.

REFLECTION

1. Write down a list of at least three people who you should use as mentors to review your potential options. Pray for them and ask them to help you discern God's will for your future. I recommend that you finish that list before continuing!

2. Spend time with each person explaining your past experiences, the way they have affected you, and the potential options for responding to them. Be open and honest in your communication. Be humble and attentive in your listening. Remember, God has often spoken through the voice of a human.

E. Decide and Commit

Let's take a moment to review what you have done thus far. You spent considerable time looking backward in order to name how you saw God, others, and yourself through your experiences. Next you tried to find a common thread that connects those experiences, discerning how God might be communicating with you. This led you to focus on what deep desires were being stirred by your experiences and to contemplate how you might nurture those desires. As you began to imagine ways in which those desires could play out in life, you spent time in prayer for the proper attitude and wisdom. As you continued the process, you looked externally for guidance in Scripture and community. By now, hopefully you have some concrete ideas of how to move from the experiences of the past to the ministry of the future.

For some, you will have one very clear idea of how you should respond. It will seem that the choice is obvious—not only to you but also to those around you. If this is the case, then be grateful.

For others, reaching the ultimate decision is not as easy. You might need to slow down and spend even more time in prayer, Scripture, and community. Perhaps there are people you have not consulted with who can give you key insights. Perhaps you are ignoring viable options because your mind was made up before you started. Perhaps you just need to give the decision a little more time to sink into your heart.

> For many people, that is easier said than done. Instead of stepping out in confidence, we struggle to step out at all. Indecision and hesitation paralyze us.

At some point, you must make a decision on how to proceed. As I mentioned earlier, "proceeding" for you might mean jumping into new ministry opportunities, committing to spiritual growth in certain areas, participating more intimately in community, or striking out on a new career path. Whatever the implication, the key at this point is to commit to moving forward.

Yet, for many people, that is easier said than done. Instead of stepping out in confidence, we struggle to step out at all. Indecision and hesitation paralyze us.

There are many factors that contribute to this, but the fact is that clicking on the "submit" button in real life is terrifying. Take surfing or shopping around on the Internet: it is often fun to click the mouse and visit many and various options, checking them out. But to click it that last time, to make that purchase, or commitment, often feels like a "point of no return." It is the same thing with a huge life decision—only amplified. What if I make a poor decision? What if I read too much into the situation and misunderstood? What if these decisions move me further away from what others have expected of me? What if . . . what if?

One of the most common metaphors in Scripture—remember, Scripture was written to teach about the nature of God and a relationship with him—is God as a parent. There are plenty of metaphors of God as father and mother. He cares for his children deeply; he calls us things like treasured possessions and the apple of his

> I am much more interested in them than I am in what they *do*.

eye. As the father of four, I know my children will make some great decisions and some bad ones. Just because they may or may not choose well when it comes to how to spend their lives, where to go to school, what major to pursue, or whom to marry does not mean that I will walk away from them if they goof. As a father, I love my children and want a lifelong relationship with them.

That relationship takes priority over any decision they could make. I am much more interested in them than I am in what they *do*.

God is no different. His primary concern is a deep relationship with you like he had when he walked in the garden with Adam and Eve or when he walked in the garden with Peter, James, and John. Relationship is his priority; let it be yours.

With that concept in mind, understand also that parents hate seeing their children agonize over little things. I hate watching one of my kids spend excess energy on what a friend will think about how they dress. On the other hand, I love spending time just talking with them and watching them grow.

Have confidence that God is like a parent and not like your computer. When you make a decision, he will not send you a pop-up message saying, "This action is permanent and cannot be undone. Are you sure you want to proceed?" If you have done your best to listen to him through experience, prayer, Scripture, and community, then he will be pleased with your efforts. And a parent is always pleased when their child tries hard, regardless of whether they finish first or last in the race.

Goal 5: Decide and Commit

Trust that God is your parent, someone who loves you. You've sought him through experience, prayer, Scripture, and community. What is he calling you to at this point in your life?

So what will it be? What do you think God wants you to get from this experience? How should you proceed? Go ahead: click the "submit" button in your spiritual life.

REFLECTION

1. Now that you have spent time naming past experiences and contemplating how to build on them through Ignatian principles, make a commitment to the option that seems most appropriate to you and your community.

2. Write down your commitment and plan as a pledge that can serve to keep you accountable to what you have decided.

Chapter 7

MISSIONS AND MINISTRY

Though you might be reading this book for multiple reasons, it was originally written for those who have just experienced significant missions, ministry, and/ or cross-cultural service. We all have experiences that move us to re-examine our lives; very often those experiences are related to serving others, the heart of missions and ministry.

The experiences that brought you to this point have been formative for multiple reasons. As a person seeking to please God, your commitment to his kingdom placed you in a different role than you have ever played. As a student serving cross-culturally, you were not in control of much of your life; you were more vulnerable than is normal. As a learner, you were open to observing and listening to people(s) in more intense ways than usual.

It is possible that using this workbook has brought you to a commitment to missions; if so, then this section might help you flesh out the next steps. However, it is also quite possible that the process has caused you to focus more on personal or spiritual characteristics in your life. If the latter is closer to your situation, then this is also a great opportunity to consider how to continue placing yourself in missions and/ or ministry opportunities that can fan into flame the fire that has been kindled inside you.

> At the end of their summer, he wisely explained to them, "If you really want to know if you are cut out for the missionary life, consider coming to work with us for a year after you graduate."

Wimon Walker, a man who has dedicated his life to cross-cultural ministry and the cofounder of World-Wide Witness internships at Abilene Christian University, was living with his family in Botswana when he first hosted summer interns. At the end of their summer, he wisely explained to them, "If you really want to know if you are cut out for the missionary life, consider coming to work with us for a year after you graduate." It was a great challenge and a wise idea.

Many mission interns have accepted Wimon's challenge to serve abroad for a year after graduation. This concept of a "lag year" between school and the working world is becoming more and more common. You might consider the option of graduating and then returning to the site where you just served. Similarly, you might spend time with mentors (like the directors of your program) to consider if another location might be more appropriate for you because of what you have just learned about God, others, and self.

If you are an underclassman, a post-graduation lag year might seem incomprehensible at the moment. Many students in your situation have chosen to take advantage of their remaining summers to repeat their service as interns. Some felt so connected with the people they left behind that they quickly committed to a second summer internship in the same location. Others felt that they should change locations because of what they learned through their recent experiences.

Still other students felt led to long-term missions/ ministry. You might consider joining an existing work, inquiring about teams in formation, or pulling together your network of close friends to form a mission/ministry team for future work in church planting, youth work, campus ministry, holistic ministry, social justice, sports ministry, etc.

The options seem endless, but your need for direction is more immediate. Take a minute now to consider how to keep yourself in a place where God is at work.

REFLECTION

1. How will you place yourself in missions/ministry opportunities that will allow you to continue to be formed and used by God? What could you do during the school year, summer, or post-graduation? If you feel you are lacking insight, then take this question to your friends/mentors listed in Chapter 6.

2. Write out how you propose to stay involved in missions/ministry. Put this written commitment somewhere you will see it frequently—mirror, phone, calendar, or other similar places.

Chapter 8

FEEDBACK

When I was a young man, I felt that I was intelligent and particularly apt at making good decisions. On a date with a young lady I'll call Ellen, I had decided to go to a nice restaurant and then to the park for a walk. As we drove from campus to the restaurant, I knew exactly where I was going and therefore was able to relax and engage in conversation. After a few minutes I noticed Ellen seemed a little uptight. When I asked what she was thinking, she replied that she thought I had missed the turn to the restaurant. I assured her that I knew where I was going and not to worry. A few minutes later she again commented that she was pretty sure the restaurant was now behind us.

"No problem," I said. "It's really just a little farther down the road."

It was about that time that I noticed a sign that read "Interstate 12" rather than what I needed, Interstate 10. *Hmmm. That's odd,* I thought. *I must have mixed the two in my head. Since I know I'm on the right road, it is obvious that I just incorrectly remembered the interstate number.* And so I kept driving.

Several minutes and a lot of conversation later, I noticed another odd sign. It was the exit for O'Neal Lane. Suddenly my brain could not process what was happening. I struggled internally to recall where O'Neal Lane crosses the interstate I was supposed to be on. The answer was: It didn't!

I glanced over at Ellen, who had a silly grin on her face. She gently replied, "I really don't think we are going the right way." My sense of pride turned into a deep feeling of stupidity, and my confidence melted faster than my ice cream did at the

> The moral of the story is simply this: stay open to feedback even after you make a decision. The feedback may be negative, like the feedback I had on my date. It may also come in a positive form of affirmation.

restaurant later that night.

The moral of the story is simply this: stay open to feedback even after you make a decision. The feedback may be negative, like the feedback I had on my date— but that just might be the feedback you need. It may also come in a positive form of affirmation as God and others facilitate the nurturing of your decision.

When my wife and I discerned that we needed to move back to the states from Venezuela, we committed ourselves fully to the plan. Despite the decision being an excruciating one, we were bolstered by the amazing amount of affirmation we received along the way. Our home sold within four weeks, at market value, and without a Realtor, while three other houses in the neighborhood had been on the market for more than eighteen months. When the paperwork for selling our cars hit a major government obstacle the week before our departure, a phenomenal series of events led to an Army commander ordering his corporal to process my paperwork while I sat in his air-conditioned office (and all without asking for a bribe!). When we investigated job opportunities in the states, five options landed in our laps in less than

> Though the discernment process had led us to choose a painful path, the affirmation along the way gave us confidence that the decision was a good one.

a week. Though the discernment process had led us to choose a painful path, the affirmation along the way gave us confidence that the decision was a good one.

Now that you have committed yourself to a plan of action, keep your spiritual ears open for feedback. God will not stop communicating just because you have completed an experience or phase of life. As Jesus said over and over: "He who has ears to hear, let him hear."

REFLECTION

1. What are ways that you have received spiritual feedback in your life? List the different avenues that God has used to give you feedback after a decision.

2. Obviously, you can't know the exact details of how you will hear from God, nor how you will need to respond. You can, however, make a commitment to listen carefully and respond appropriately. Take a moment to write out a pledge to receive and respond to spiritual feedback.

EPILOGUE

Much more could be written about good decision making and the will of God. This short work is simply written to help you process a recent ministry, mission, and/or cross-cultural experience. In the future, you will face many more opportunities to discern the will of God for your life. Hopefully, this little book will be helpful to you at those times as well.

> *[Be] confident of this, that he who began a good work in you will carry it on to completion until the day of Christ Jesus.* PHILIPPIANS 1:6

May our Father in Heaven bless and guide you as you seek to become more like him.

MORE RESOURCES ON DISCERNMENT

Barton, Ruth Halley. *Sacred Rhythms: Arranging Our Lives for Spiritual Transformation.* Downers Grove, IL: InterVarsity, 2006. Print.

Bracken, Joseph A. "God's Will or God's Desires for Us: A Change in Worldview." *Theological Studies* 71.1 (2010): 62-78. Print.

Calhoun, Adele Ahlberg. *Spiritual Disciplines Handbook: Practices That Transform Us.* Downers Grove, IL: InterVarsity, 2005. Print.

Cary, Phillip. "No Secret Plan: Why You Don't Have to Find God's Will for Your Life." *The Christian Century.* 20-23, 21 Sept. 2010. Web. 8 June 2011. <http://www.christiancentury.org/article/2010-09/no-secret-plan>.

Friesen, Garry, and J. Robin Maxson. *Decision Making & the Will of God: A Biblical Alternative to the Traditional View.* Portland, OR: Multnomah, 1980. Print.

Hamm, Dennis, SJ. "Rummaging for God: Praying Backwards Through Your Day." *Ignatian Spirituality.* Web. 28 Feb. 2013. <http://www.ignatianspirituality. com/ignatian-prayer/the-examen/rummaging-for-god-praying-backward-through-your-day/>.

Horton, Dennis J., PhD. "Discerning Spiritual Discernment: Assessing Current Approaches for Understanding God's Will." *Journal of Youth Ministry* Spring 7.2 (2009): 7-31. Print.

LaReau, Renée M. "Give Me a Sign: How Do I Know I'm Doing God's Will?" *USCatholic.org.* 12-17, 26 June 2008. Web. 16 Mar. 2011. <http://www.uscatholic. org/life/2008/07/give-me-a-sign>.

Lay, Liberty. "How Do I Know God's Will? Four Big Questions We All Ask." *Christianity Today.* 32-33, Web. 1 Apr. 2011. <http://www.christianitytoday.com/ iyf/hottopics/faithvalues/godswill.html?start=1>.

Pinnock, Clark H. *The Openness of God: A Biblical Challenge to the Traditional Understanding of God.* Downers Grove, IL: InterVarsity, 1994. Print.

Thibodeaux, Mark E. *God's Voice Within: The Ignatian Way to Discover God's Will.* Chicago: Loyola, 2010. Print.

WORLDWIDE WITNESS

WORLDWIDE
WI†NESS

In 2001, following mission work in Venezuela, the author partnered with Wimon Walker to found the WorldWide Witness program (WWW) for the Halbert Institute for Missions at Abilene Christian University. Since that date, the author and co-director Larry Henderson have recruited, trained and sent more than 650 short-term workers to the mission field.

WWW is designed to be more than the typical one to two-week experience that is now common among North American evangelicals. The program typically places students for an average of two months on the field. Some, however, stay for as long as two years.

Students who are accepted to the program are interviewed and the directors attempt to find the best "fit" for the student depending upon his/her gifts and desires. Training is conducted through a formal class in the spring semester entitled Service in Global Contexts. Topics covered include spiritual disciplines, cultural sensitivity, fundraising, worldviews, mission principles and more. At the end of the class, students travel to their host destinations in small teams of two or three. While working hand-in-hand with local Christians, the teams live with national hosts or missionaries and engage in a wide variety of experiences ranging from youth ministry to orphan care to agriculture.

Now What? Spiritual Discernment for Cultural Encounters was developed as a debriefing guide for WWW students.

For more information on WWW, go to
worldwidewitness.org.

NOTES